The Four Pillars of Success

I0169469

The No BS Way to an Awesome Life of Achievement

By BRIAN CARSON

Dedication

This book is dedicated to the two most important people in my life: my wife Maria and my Mom, Ada. Without my Mom I wouldn't be here and without my wife, I'd never would have achieved all that I have in my life. I love you both with all my heart.

http://marketownership.com

Contents

Introduction..6

Pillar One: Know What You Want...............................11

Pillar Two: Focus..23

Pillar Three: Action..35

Pillar Four: Persistence..46

Chapter 5: Gratitude & Giving...................................55

Chapter 6: Good Health..65

Chapter 7: Putting it All Together..............................83

Epilogue..99

Introduction

This book came about because of the misinformation that's running rampant in the self-improvement industry. Most of this is unintentional.

Anyone involved in any kind of success coaching, this author included, has borrowed heavily from the past and what's gone down before. Not a problem there. If something is true and significant, others should incorporate it.

Unfortunately, in an effort to make a fast buck some have misinterpreted self-help and science, in particular quantum physics, into this new age hocus pocus that states all you have to do is chant affirmations, visualize and all your dreams will come true.

Don't worry about taking action or doing anything else for that matter. Just affirm and visualize and it will come to you. Sorry to be the one to tell you this, but that's a bunch of crap.

Anyone and I do mean anyone that says you can achieve all your dreams and have whatever you want in a matter of months is a liar. Run as far away as you can from them and the pack of lies they're dishing out.

Selling the notion of instantaneous results without effort is out and out irresponsible and downright criminal in some instances. The promise of microwaveable instant success is the result of the I-have-to-have-it-now fast food generation.

Forget about planning, preparation and patient, consistent action. The "Get Rich Quick" mantra is a lie spoon-fed to the masses. Advertisers created it after a fast buck.

I have to be straight with you. I know of no other way to be. Achieving anything worthwhile takes effort. You have to pay the price to reach your goals. It won't come to you on a silver platter without any work on your part.

Affirmations and visualization are important to successful living. I am all for them. However, you must learn to use them in their proper context. And you will here. If you're looking for get rich quick schemes or some new age junk, stop right now - this **is not** for you.

But if you want to learn the true way to attainment, the principles one must follow to achieve lasting success, then this book is for you. I've spent the last 26 years studying every bit of information in the self-improvement field.

My research has led me to what you're reading now - the four principles that lead to lasting success and achievement - however you define those terms. I call them the four pillars, because they are the foundation of every success you'll ever have.

Surprised? I hope so. You see you don't have to memorize 21 or 52 success secrets that really aren't secrets at all. Authors who say you must maintain a positive attitude at all times are living in a fantasy world. No one and I mean no one; can have a positive attitude all the time. How can you be positive if there's a death in the family or a loved one is ill? You can't.

One of the founding principles in the self-improvement field since its huge growth in the early 20th century has been the doctrine that you must never have a negative thought.

All negative thoughts need purged and replaced with only harmonious, positive, happy thoughts. So the experts say.

If anyone has seriously tried to do this, you'll notice a problem right away. It's damn hard to think positive all the time! This has caused individuals undue frustration.

Many think something is wrong with them and they're not good enough. So they give up trying to improve themselves and stay stuck in second gear.

This creates a cycle of doubt, fear and frustration. All caused by a self-improvement book that's supposed to be helping them! It's a rather strange dichotomy wouldn't you agree?

Well, I'm here to break this cycle once and for all. Yes, you can have a negative thought and yes, you can still achieve tremendous success even if you have negative thoughts. The key is to limit them. Stop the ones that you can stop and roll with the punches on the ones you can't.

As long as we are alive on this earth there are going to be times when things go wrong. Nobody is immune to problems. Some have the illusion that money solves all problems. Sorry kiddies. It's not true.

Problems will come and they'll come in many forms: death in the family, relationships, business setbacks, health and of course the biggie for most people - lack of funds from time to time.

Problems come and problems go. It's a natural cycle that never changes. Only through adversity do we have the chance to grow, learn and come out the other side better than we were before.

Trust me on this. No matter how bad it looks, if you persevere and hang on, you will grow and prosper from the experience. Bad things do happen to good people and it's okay to be negative once in a while when you're going through those times. We're only human after all.

The key is to eliminate negative thoughts that just randomly pop into your head when things are going smoothly. Those you have to eliminate immediately. Replace them with a positive thought right away. Because if you don't it could develop into a lifetime pattern of negative thinking.

Focus on your goals. Keep your eye on the prizes that you've set for yourself. Do this during the good, normal and bad times that will come during a lifetime of living. And in the end, everything will be fine. The key is never giving up and staying focused on what you want to create in your life.

Therefore, when problems arise, it's not a crime to have negative thoughts. Just keep persisting. Learn what the adversity has to teach you and move on to greener pastures.

It's impossible to be positive all the time. Only through struggle, adversity and strain do we learn and grow. You take the lessons life teaches, learn from them, and become a better individual and move on to a higher level.

In all my years of research studying high achievers in business, the arts, government and various religions - the four principles here presented were used by all of them. Without exception!

The key word is use. Knowledge is power only if it's applied. If you just skim through this book and don't USE or apply the principles contained - you'll get nothing from this. But if you USE and act on what you learn, the world will be your oyster. It will open up and give you all its pearls.

Take care. God Bless and I hope you achieve all the success I know can be yours.

Brian Carson
Lewistown, PA
2013

PILLAR ONE: Know What You Want

"When you know what you want, and want it bad enough, you will find a way to get it."

Jim Rohn

All Achievement Begins with a Definite Purpose

Imagine taking your family on a trip across the country without a GPS or map and no idea where you're going. Pretty stupid isn't it - going to and fro with no plans, destination or goals in mind. You could end up anywhere from Boston to California and all points in between.

Surprisingly, the majority of individuals on this big, blue marble known as earth - do the same thing when it comes to building their lives. As a matter of fact, most have a more detailed plan of a family vacation then they do a career.

Without a definite purpose and a plan to reach it, you're destined for failure. If you don't know what you want, how can you ever hope to accomplish anything?

Life is a marvelous experience. It's supposed to be that way. We can have what we want in our short speck of time allotted to us, but we have to know what it is before we can reach it. Speak your desires, claim your inheritance and get what is rightfully yours.

The first pillar to ultimate success is this - **know what you want**. It seems so simple and you've probably read it a million times, but the truth is always eternal. There is nothing new under the sun when it comes to fundamental, spiritual laws. You just have to open your eyes and ears and understand.

The oak tree knows it's an oak tree and what its purpose is - to give shelter, shade and produce more oak trees. The grass feeds the animals and produces more grass. Everything is growth and abundance in nature. We are to grow and be prosperous - provided we know our purpose.

We are goal-oriented organisms. The only time a human being really thrives and expands is in pursuit of a goal. It's what drives us and makes life complete. Even during the inevitable struggle that must be overcome to achieve our purpose - we are at our most highly charged. We are the most creative. We are alive.

Decide What You Want - Now!

Don't wait until the time is right or perfect. That's a myth. Now is the only right time. Decide what you want. Think about it intently and carefully. This is the most important decision anyone can ever make. Create it. Don't let circumstances allow you to drift towards a life of mediocrity. Find your purpose, go after your goals and make your destiny.

If you're having problems, creating goals here are some helpful tips and questions to ask yourself:

* Write down your hobbies, what fills you with passion.
* What would you do even if you didn't get paid for it?
* What talents do you have? Get a loved one to help if you're not sure.
* Ask yourself, 'what would I do if I knew I could not fail? Write it down.
* Fantasize. Use your imagination and create your perfect life. Write it down.

Once you have a list of goals, rank them in order of importance and begin immediately to create plans for their attainment.

Don't worry if your plans are not complete. Don't worry if you haven't a clue how to accomplish them. The important thing is to start. Eventually, if you are truly serious, your subconscious mind will show you the path to take.

One way to start is education. If you have a goal of being an oceanographer, but don't know the first thing about ocean life - then studying oceanography is a must. Education and study are required even if you've reached expert status in your field.

Never stop learning new ways of doing things. Never stop your education. If you do, the mind shrivels and become useless. You must always have that fire for learning and believe me, if a subject enthralls you - the passion for learning more about it will come naturally.

Now more than ever, information on any topic is easily found. From the Internet, to mega-bookstores to libraries, knowledge abounds in many forms and places.

Any kind of knowledge that can make you a better person is of paramount importance to developing character. Studying some of the great thinkers, writers and philosophers from the past can only be beneficial to the person who pursues them.

Whatever is uplifting is good. Never stop trying to improve, to be better and to mold your character. Reading these masters will develop self-confidence and the positive attitudes needed to fight off and solve problems when they do come.

We learn through repetition, association and emotion. Using these principles, if you keep studying success philosophy, it's only natural that the constant bombardment of positive ideas and principles will have a beneficial effect on the individual. It may take time to seep into your subconscious, but rest assured, it will.

Biography, philosophy, positive psychology and uplifting stories should be a success student's prime material of study. Through this material and life experiences an individual will form the strength of will and character needed to overcome any roadblocks along the way.

There is a goldmine of material for you to devour in your quest for a better life. Take advantage of the wealth of information available for you to study. Absorb the principles that you learn and apply them. If you do, you'll find that life can be a truly wonderful experience.

The Power of Decision

Deciding to decide is one of the most powerful tools nature gives humanity. The true successful leaders of the world are quick to decide and slow to change their minds.

Indecision is a disease that needs to be eradicated. Failure to make up your mind will cause irreparable damage that can have life-long consequences. Indecision is right up there with self-doubt as the number one cause for lack of success. This shouldn't happen. Deciding to decide is a relatively simple concept.

First, get a definite major purpose and create some smaller goals that will lead you to your major one. After figuring out what you want, make all your decisions based on those goals. If a choice will take you further from the goal, don't do it. If it leads you closer to the goal, take action right away.

Indecision creates anxiety, depression and leaves the indecisive person in a pool of inertia that's very hard to break free from. Each time a decision is put off; the problem gets bigger and bigger. It's like trying to drain the Atlantic Ocean with a teacup.

The way out is by deciding. Make a choice and follow the path. Be slow to change, but don't be so rigid that you can't see the forest for the trees. After a decent period of time, if the choice you've made isn't working, go and try something else.

So if you're stuck in a rut and aren't sure where to go, decide to decide and that will set in motion forces to help you along the way. Decisiveness has power in the act itself. When you know what you want and make the decisions that will bring you closer to your goals, life magically falls into place.

Here are five steps to becoming more decisive in your life:

1. Find your definite purpose
2. Only make decisions that will lead you closer to your goals
3. Once a decision is made, be slow to change and quick to act
4. If a decision doesn't work out after a period of time, stop and go another way
5. Wash, rinse and repeat

Follow these five steps and you'll be a quality decision maker in no time.

IDEAS

We all have ideas. The difference is in how you deal with them, Winners take action on their ideas. If they're not good, they toss them out and move on to the next. Others fail because they give up, procrastinate or lack confidence in their ideas. Action is key. Don't set around and wait for ideas to come, be a doer and follow the following six steps.

The Six Steps to Creating Powerful Ideas

1. Believe that you're an idea generator - We all know by now the power of the mind. Success in anything relies upon belief. Creativity is a learned process. You have to believe that you're creative and the ideas will come. It takes work to develop this ability, but it can be done. Let it sink into your subconscious and most of all relax. Ideas come when you least expect them to.

2. Creativity and idea generation must be practiced - The only way to become proficient and develop skill in any endeavor is to practice until it becomes second nature. Ideas and creativity are no different. Have lots of ideas, experiment with them and if some are bad, move on to the next and the next. Try new things and react quickly. To become an idea machine - practice, practice, practice!

3. Have a system to record your ideas - Ideas are slippery things, if you don't write them down right away, they have a tendency to disappear rather quickly. Always keep a notebook, index cards or a voice recorder handy to record those sudden flashes of inspiration that always pop up in unexpected places and times. Don't forget to analyze your ideas after you record them. If it's just a to-do list type of item, drop it from your idea journal.

4. Sit for Ideas - This is a principle taken directly from Think and Grow Rich. Scientist and inventor Elmer Gates told Napoleon Hill how he came up with many of his ideas and creations. He stated that he would go into a small room with just a table, chair and sometimes turn out the lights and sit for hours waiting for flashes of inspiration to come. When it did, he'd quickly turn on the lights and write down his ideas. Follow his example, go to place where you feel most comfortable and can be alone (you don't have to turn out any lights) and wait for ideas. It can be anywhere. Einstein's place for ideas was his shower.

5. Be around other idea people - These can be your friends, family or co-workers. To be creative, hang around creative people. Form your own mastermind group and meet weekly to brainstorm or discuss each other's ideas. Creativity thinking begets more creativity thinking.

6. Look for ideas outside your industry, business, field or interest - Always look for ideas and creative thinking outside your area of interest. Borrow ideas from others and remake them as your own - do it better, improve upon it and apply it to your field.

Remember that ideas that can save time and money, solve problems and make money will always be needed. Focus on them and get your just rewards.

Get your specialized education if needed to implement your ideas. If you become discouraged don't forget - most ideas are a combination of borrowing with some originality thrown in for good measure. They are borrowed ideas rearranged. Very few are truly 100 percent original. Arm yourself with this information, use it, act on it and achieve.

Establish Your Ultimate Goal

What do you want?

- ➢ Are you looking for financial security, professional acknowledgment, and spiritual attainment?

- ➢ Do you want to fit better socially, or become more expressive creatively?

Establish the goal that's right for you.

Then turn that goal from a dream into a desire.

You want to realize the goal, not just wish for it.

Aesop said, *"Beware that you do not lose the substance by grabbing at the shadow."*

Know exactly what you want, then go for it.

Don't be robbed by your own procrastination- <u>especially</u> if you want to achieve something unique or original...artistic.

The writer Thomas Wolfe wrote, *"I had been sustained by that delightful illusion of success which we all have when we dream about the books we are going to write instead of actually doing them."*

He went on to say, *"Now I was face to face with it, and suddenly I realized that I had committed my life and my integrity so irrevocably to this struggle that I must conquer now or be destroyed."*

Can you see - with complete **clarity** - what you want?

If you want the abundance of material wealth that money provides, what goal will give you that money?

- ✓ Do you want the prestige of owning your own business?

- ✓ What business do you want to begin?

- ✓ Where are the opportunities for you?

18

Talk to everyone in the business you want to join. Make friends in the literary or art societies in your area. Read books and articles about your field of endeavor. How can you attain your goal?

"If you don't want to work, you have to work to earn enough money so that you don't have to work," wrote Ogden Nash. And, isn't that the way:

Money *makes* Money; Success *breeds* Success.

How can you break through those thoughts to help yourself to the rewards?

Henry David Thoreau wrote...

"I have learned this at least by my experiment: that if you advance confidently in the direction of your dreams, and endeavor to live the life which you imagine, you will meet with success unexpected in common hours."

Think big and visualize success:

➜ Do you see yourself in a big house?

➜ Maybe you picture your artwork hanging in a gallery.

➜ Can you feel your book in print and in your hands?

➜ How does it feel to be a person of success?!?

Make firm that you are; know it is in your grasp. That's what most of the greats have done, and that's how people make it to the top. Then get down to basics. Be precise.

➜ Exactly how much money do you want and do you have a plan laid out to get it?

➜ And exactly what are you going to do to earn that

money?

Be realistic, but give yourself short-term goals. Write it down.

In six months or one year, you will have *how much* money. Visualize and repeat it until it feels good...natural and normal...at least twice a day until it swirls in your subconscious, until it becomes your **single-pointed** goal.

"The goal stands up, the keeper stands up to keep the goal" wrote A.E. Housman.

An Important Key to Goal Attainment

Do you want a super fast, practically guaranteed way to reach your goals? This one technique has been used repeatedly by the top achievers throughout history and is still used by many millionaires and billionaires today.

It was first written about in a little tome by R.H. Jarrett titled, 'It Works.' A main proponent of this method today is self-help guru Brian Tracy. As a matter of fact, he credits his application of this principle as the single most important reason for his success.

What is this simple little technique that has helped many high achievers reach their goals? It is the habit of **WRITING DOWN YOUR GOALS DAILY!**

That's it, nothing earth-shatteringly difficult to do. Every morning when you first wake up and every evening before you go to bed, write your goals down in the positive, present tense as if you've already achieved them.

The positive, present tense is important. Don't use I will or I want. It must be stated as if the goal is already achieved. Instead of affirming, "I will make $50,000 a year," say, "I make or I earn $50,000 a year."

"I want a Mercedes Benz S-Class," becomes "I drive a

Mercedes Benz S-Class."

Don't put a time limit on goals. Many self-improvement authors urge people to do so, but it's wrong. Placing your goals in a future time that does not exist cannot possibly bring results. There is only the ever-present now. As hard a concept as it is to grasp, there's only now. The past and the future do not exist.

When you think of the past, when are you thinking of it? Now. When you think of the future, when are you thinking of it? Now. When you arrive at the future, when will it be? Now. When did you experience the events of your past? Now.

Every individual lives in the now. If you set a future date instead of now, the subconscious mind is programmed to always be looking towards a future that never comes because we're always living in the now.

So write out your goals twice a day, morning and evening. Make them in the positive, present tense and amazing things will happen. But only if you have grasped and applied the First Pillar of Success - **Know What You Want.**

PILLAR TWO:
Focus

Gather in your resources, rally all your faculties, marshal all your energies, focus all your capacities upon mastery of at least one field of endeavor.

John Haggai

Of all the success principles taught, none has been more misunderstood than visualization.

The current state of the self-help field teaches us to visualize every morning and night and your goal will attract itself to you. Sorry, but that just isn't the case.

Visualization is a tool, an important one of course, but you have to do more than just visualize. Sorry people, but the success game is a little bit more complicated than that. The universe requires you to earn your way, to prove you have the muster and gumption to deserve your goals.

What you sow, you reap. In other words, you must earn your way by your efforts. Visualization alone will not do it. We live in an action-oriented world and while visualization serves an important purpose, your visions and dreams must be balanced with purposeful pursuit of those goals.

The true importance of visualizing is to keep you focused on your target. Visualization should be done during every waking moment, not just at certain times.

By that, I mean you must keep your vision in your mind as you go about your day. You don't have to close your eyes, listen to music and all that stuff. Just have it there in the back of your mind to bring to recall at a moment's notice.

Focused action must be accompanied with all visualization. Otherwise, all you have is a daydream. It doesn't have to be a giant step, as long as it's some type of action that will start you on the way to acquiring what you're visualizing.

The individuals who are teaching the just visualize movement are doing a complete disservice to those pursuing the path to personal excellence. If it were easy, everyone would accomplish their wildest dreams. But as we all know, it just isn't so.

Visualization and action work synergistically to create the life of your dreams.

Visualization alone is not enough. Combine it with small action steps toward your vision and life will give you what you ask of it.

This is the true purpose for visualization and affirmation. It keeps one motivated and focused on the goal and it stimulates the subconscious to develop ways and plans for the achievement of the goal.

This is the second pillar of success – **focus or concentration**.

The Power of Focus

Self-help guru, Tony Robbins, once said, "controlled focus is like a laser beam."

If a laser didn't have a specific target to lock onto, its energy would dissipate into the atmosphere. But focus the laser on the target with enough energy and it will pass through solid steel.

Place a magnifying glass in the path of the sun's rays and you have a powerful force at work. That is pure, concentrated focus at its best. Such is the power of controlled attention and why it's so important in achieving your goals.

If you are concentrating on a million things at once, there won't be enough energy to accomplish any task set before you. But, focus on only one thing and you'll involve your entire force in the completion of the goal.

All the energy an individual can muster, focused on a specific goal, can't help but make that outcome a reality. Controlled focus, backed by faith, is an incredible power that will bring you any objective you want to achieve.

It's perfectly fine to have many goals, but you must focus on them one at a time to bring all your power to their achievement. If you spread yourself thin, a goal may be accomplished, but it will take longer and with much more work needed to achieve it. If you focus on each goal, one at a time, then all your concentrated power is unleashed on the objective.

With controlled focus, one by one, all your goals will be completed. Do your tasks in order and don't be led astray by multi-tasking. Contrary to popular opinion, multi-tasking is not a good thing. Doing too many projects at once leads to stress and a lack of productivity.

Taking things one at a time reduces stress and allows the individual to put all their power to the job at hand. Focus equals higher productivity and more success. A winning combination if there ever was one.

So remember the next time you feel stressed and swamped with work. Use the power of controlled focus. Take on each project one at a time, focus on the completion of each task and watch your productivity and your success soar.

Concentration

Nothing great has ever been accomplished without concentration. The ability to focus on a goal until its completion is a main factor in all levels of achievement.

No matter what field - be it business, sports, music or public service - the power of concentration is what separates the average from the great. No matter what the talent level of the individual is.

Focusing on a goal to its completion is more important than skill level, intelligence or anything else. Concentration can make one rise from lowly beginnings to the heights of Olympus. From outhouse to penthouse, the old saying goes, and controlled focus can make it happen.

Controlled concentration takes discipline and in order to develop it, one must pick an objective or goal that will fire the imagination and stir the soul. When the goal is decided upon, then all your energy, mental and physical, needs to be directed to the attainment of the goal.

Look neither left nor right, up or down and to the side. The whole force of your being should be looking in one direction - straight ahead. That is the key. Never deviate from the path, concentrate all your efforts towards the goal and in time the objective will be yours.

Stay focused, keep concentrating. If you do this, all obstacles and circumstances will bow before you. Concentration along with belief and action is a triple-threat combination that can't be defeated.

Belief shows the path, concentration keeps you on course and action brings your desires to you. The more you practice the better you become. Don't be frustrated when you start. Keep on trying and you'll become a master. Apply your power of focus to a worthwhile end and great things will happen in your life.

Thoughts are things and what you think about expands. If you learn to harness your mental energy towards a goal, excluding everything else, you can't help but receive the desired outcome. It is a mental law that never deviates.

Decide on a goal. Use your powers of concentration to focus on the goal to the exclusion of all else. Finally, take action towards the objective and the world will acquiesce to your mental demands.

Imagination

The importance of imagination in the achievement of goals can't and shouldn't be overlooked. Albert Einstein once said that imagination is more important than knowledge. Even the Holy Bible mentions the unbelievable power of this mental faculty.

In the eleventh chapter of Genesis, the sixth verse states, "And the Lord said behold the people is one and they all have one language; and this they begin to do: *And now nothing will be restrained from them, which they have imagined to do.*"

Did you get that? Can you fully grasp the awesome possibilities in the previous statement? Read it again and again until it seeps into your deeper consciousness. It's that important. There's no reason people need fail in any endeavor. The excuses are officially over.

Nothing will be restrained from them means just that. Anything you want can be yours as long as it doesn't violate the laws of God or man. The key is the imagined to do part. Imagined is visualization - the creation of a mental picture of an as-yet-to-happen event.

So the gist of the passage in Genesis is whatever you visualize with consistency and belief, will become reality in your life, provided you take action.

This is the tremendous, awesome power of your imagination in full bloom.

Everyone has it within them to make their imagination create the life they envision, but few make an attempt or even understand the tremendous power between their ears. It's really very simple - decide what you want, visualize it constantly, believe it will happen, let your subconscious show you the way and take persistent, focused action until the objective is achieved.

The correct use of the imagination has been a prime reason for the success of individuals in all callings and endeavors.

Business titans like Andrew Carnegie, John D. Rockefeller and Sam Walton have tapped into this power. Julius Caesar, Alexander the Great and Ghengis Kahn made use of their imaginations to become world conquerors. Closer to home - a bevy of sports stars, actors and ordinary people from all walks of life - have achieved incredible success by harnessing the power of the imagination.

Learn the correct use of your imagination; your visualizing muscle, and the universe will give you your hearts desires. God has endowed every one of us with this incredible gift - the ability to picture in our minds something we want to happen - knowing that one always moves in the direction of their dominant thoughts.

Live life letting circumstances drift you to and fro with no clear-cut purpose or destination. Or harness the awesome power of your imagination and create the life you desire. The choice as always is yours.

Why You Need a Burning Desire to Succeed

As Napoleon Hill said so succinctly, "a burning desire is the starting point of all riches." Your definite purpose must be fused with a burning desire in order for the universe to acquiesce to your demands.

Without a burning desire, without passion for the objective you're trying to reach, only a half-hearted effort will be put forward for its attainment. And a half-hearted effort will accomplish very little.

Only an all-out focused effort will bring you the objectives you seek and the only way to create this all-out effort is by enveloping your definite purpose with a burning passion. Mix those ingredients with concentrated thought and confident action and the whole universe will bow to your wishes.

How do you acquire a burning desire? With tools already in your arsenal – imagination, affirmation and knowledge of what drives you.

Decide what you really want, visualize its attainment over and over and over again with feeling and finally, affirm constantly that you really want this and you will achieve it. Before long, you will create a burning desire so white hot, that nothing will be able to stop you.

The desire should be so strong that it's the first thing you think about in the morning and the last thing you think about before going to sleep. It should dominate your thoughts. You may have

29

other things to do during your day, but after completing those tasks, your burning desire should be front and center in your conscious mind.

A burning desire, backed by faith, allows you to go through the difficult times knowing in the end, you will emerge victorious. A burning desire, backed by faith, allows you to move forward, no matter what the cost, to reach your objective. A burning desire, backed by faith, is the strongest force in the universe.

An important side note: Your burning desire should be something of a positive nature. If your desire is to hurt someone, gain something through illegal means, or cause any injury at all, you will pay a heavy price. Remember cause and effect. What you sow you reap, so only desire things that can benefit yourself and mankind in a positive way.

If you follow the above rule, visualize and affirm your intention with feeling, you will create a burning desire that will sweep all obstacles and problems out of your way. A burning desire is the starting point of all achievement. You can develop one even if you don't have it right now. Trust me, it's well worth the effort.

The Four Keys to Creating a Burning Desire

Developing a white-hot burning desire for the attainment of a goal is one of the prerequisites of its eventual achievement. Yet some, no matter how hard they try, can't seem to work up that kind of intense passion for a goal.

Is this a problem you have? Do you feel frustrated when you read books or articles stating that a burning desire is the starting point of all achievement and yet you can't seem to ignite the flame of desire for a definite object?

If you answered yes to these questions, don't be upset. You're not alone. All of us at one time or another had trouble creating a burning desire inside.

But we need this passion in our lives, because in the long run, we only get what we truly desire and expect. A desire makes you reach higher, aspire farther and push harder to get the things you want out of life. You can accomplish anything in life if you have the burning desire to get it.

But how to develop that kind of desire? It takes some effort, some persistence and constant practice on your part, but if you follow these four principles, a burning desire for your goals can and will be a part of your life.

The Four Keys to Creating a Burning Desire

1. **Visualization** - You must create a sustained and lasting picture of the thing you want. Constant picturing or visualization is the first key to the attainment of your desires. Nothing has ever existed that wasn't first thought in the mind and since we think in pictures, this is the most important step to master in the creation and fulfillment of burning desire.

2. **Affirmations** - Back in the early part of the 20th century, French psychologist Dr. Emile Coue proved that repeated affirmations have a profound effect on human behavior and actions. Affirmations of your desires combined with visualization make a potent pair in creating that burning desire needed to succeed. Make sure your affirmations are stated in the present tense with emotion.

3. **Controlled Focus** - Concentration is the third key to creating a burning desire. You must give all your attention to one thing at a time. When it's time to work, go to work and when it's time to play, don't think about anything but playing. There's an old saying that goes, "it's better to complete one worthwhile goal than to begin ten others." When it comes to creating a burning desire for your goal - focus on one goal only. If you do, success is practically assured.

4. **Relationships** - This is the hardest key to get under control because of family and friends. Your own family can de-motivate you and even though their intentions may be honorable, it can

have a dramatic effect on your life. Associate with individuals who are positive and encouraging. While you don't want to announce your goals to everyone, there are associates that can keep you motivated when things aren't going well. Cultivate those types of friendships.

There you have it. The four keys to creating a burning desire are now yours. What you do with them and how you use them are totally under your control. Practice them and develop your burning desire - the starting point of all achievement.

Belief, Prime Mover of the Universe

Nothing is more important than faith. Belief is the key to unlocking all the abundance the universe has to offer. Without it, nothing is possible. With it, everything is within your grasp.

Without the power of faith, we would still be living in caves and hunting our food with homemade spears. Belief is the irresistible force that attracts to you the fruits of your faith. Whether you believe your life is a heaven or a hell – your faith will make the scenario a reality.

We are the sum total of our beliefs. Beliefs stem from thought and thought made the universe and everything in it. It is the prime mover – the foundation of the world. Faith and love are the two most powerful forces at mankind's disposal. Thankfully, we have the tools to develop rock-solid, mountain-moving faith.

The power of dominant thought, coupled with the correct use of affirmations, is the best way for developing lasting faith. Both dominant thought and affirmations work on the principles of repetition and association. The only ways in which a human being learns.

Persistent, dominant thought and persistent affirmations will develop in you dominant and persistent faith. The type of unstoppable faith that breaks down all obstacles and smashes all limits.

Powerful faith will not happen right away and if you expect it to, you will be very disappointed. For one thing, true belief must vanquish fear and doubt and those kinds of deep-rooted negative attitudes take time to eliminate.

What it takes is training the mind and allowing the empowering thoughts to drive down into the core of your being. After awhile, that faith will be so embedded nothing can drive it out. And when the belief becomes second nature and a part of your character, obstacles will fall be the wayside, and a true life of achievement will begin.

PILLAR THREE:
Action

Nothing happens without movement

Albert Einstein

Nothing happens without movement. That keen observation, one of many by the greatest scientist of any age, shines light on a crucial component in any study of success philosophy. The component of course is action. Nothing happens without action. A fact of science and a fact in creating the life you desire.

You can put all the success theories, principles and writers together and absorb everything they teach. However, if you don't put those lessons into action - nothing, I mean absolutely nothing, will happen in your life. One may even go backwards.

An individual may affirm, visualize and keep a positive attitude until they're blue in the face, but if they take no action towards their goals, success will run from them as fast as a rabbit runs from a wolf.

Action is the catalyst. The only difference between successful and unsuccessful people is movement. Successful people take action towards their goals and never give up until the objective is achieved. Unsuccessful people never take action because they let fear and doubt stop them in their tracks.

Focused action coupled with persistence is an unbeatable duo that can mow down any obstacle that gets in the way. Develop these and in time, nothing will be withheld from you. Action is faith in motion. It's knowing that no matter how tough the going gets, if you persist, your action (faith in motion) will bring you the fruits of your vision.

The third pillar of success is action. Thought (goal)-belief (faith)-focused action coupled with persistence. Embrace the principles that represent the achievement matrix and a whole new world of success and abundance will unfold before your eyes.

There is no big secret to success and no magical potions. Just apply and follow the known, proven principles to lasting accomplishment. That's all there is to it. Don't stress over how you're going to reach your goals. Just focus on them one at a time, visualize its achievement, believe you'll reach it and take focused, persistent action towards the goal and success is practically assured.

Follow your non-conscious urgings and your intuition. They will let you know if you're on the right path. If not, change course and go in the direction your heart takes you. You don't have to have a complete, systemized plan for reaching your goal. Just use your natural, God-given instincts and take action in the direction you're led.

Nothing happens without movement. Follow the achievement triangle, understand the Four Pillars of Success, take action towards your goal, and remember, nothing can stop you from success but yourself.

The Power of Dominant Thought

Wayne Dyer, the famous author, speaker and teacher, likes to say that what you focus on expands. Nothing could be more profound or truthful.

What you focus on expands should be a rallying cry for all who want and are willing to pay the price to live the life they imagine. We are the sum total of all our thoughts. Our dominant thoughts create the life we have lived up to this point and will create our futures as well. Make no mistake about it.

This is not some New Age hocus-pocus. This principle has been around for centuries. The Bible says, "As a man thinketh in his heart, that is what he is." Roman Emperor, Marcus Aurelius said, "a man's life is dyed by the color of his thoughts," and the Buddha commented that, "All that a man is comes from his thoughts."

All of us at one time have used this power of dominant thought, whether we realized it or not. When as I was about 12 or 13 years old, I really wanted to be a running back on my midget football team. Most of the time, I played on the offensive and defensive lines, but I set my sights on running back.

During the full three months of summer vacation, all I thought about morning, noon and night, was being the starting running back on the football team. Soon summer was over and we had our first practice. The coach asked us where we wanted to play and I said running back.

Long story short, I won the starting position in tryouts and played the entire season as the starting fullback. All from my dominant thought over the summer.

That is just a minor example of the power of dominant thought. There have been larger and grand examples throughout history, like the conquests of Alexander the Great and Genghis Khan to name a few.

The important key to remember is it must be dominant thought. Half-hearted or fleeting thoughts will not bring about the desired intent. Only a thought that consumes you, that dominates your waking moments, is strong enough to make it become a reality.

Also, the thought must be backed by consistent, focused action. I didn't set around all summer hoping to be the starting running back. I worked out, ran and new the playbook inside and out. Dominant thought was the catalyst, but action brought about the result.

Thoughts are things. Thoughts are electrical impulses and if a thought is strong enough it can reach out into the quantum field, which is also made up of various light vibrations (electrical impulses), and match you up with your desired thought. Like attracts like. This is a fact. If you couple your dominant thought with focused, confident action – life will give you whatever you ask.

How to Crush Fear Forever

It happens all too many times doesn't it? You set a goal, a target you wish to reach. In order to hit this target, you have to step outside your comfort zone and do something you've never done. What happens when you go to make the attempt?

Well, nine times out of ten it never gets done. As soon as you convince yourself to try, resistance shows up in the form of fear, which leads to doubt and in turn leads to giving up or never attempting to reach your goal.

If that's your story, don't be upset. The statistics are true. Only 10 percent of the population keeps on keeping on. Only 10 percent fight the fear and reach their destination. The good news is if you're not in the 10-percent club, you can get there. You can crush fear, resistance and march on to a successful life.

How? By realizing, once and for all, that fear is learned. It's a product of the mind and whatever is held in mind can be reprogrammed and changed. We are born with only one fear at childbirth - loud noises. Any other fears we've picked up are developed by a lack of understanding, our self-talk and what others have said to us that we've incorporated into our minds as truth.

FEAR is an acronym for 'False Evidence Appearing Real.' It doesn't exist accept in our own minds. And since we have control of only one thing in life - our thoughts. Fear can be wiped out by changing our thoughts.

The most successful people, no matter what their calling, had fears to overcome. All of us have fears and doubts. However, it doesn't have to be that way. Human beings are giants who choose to live like amoebas. The successful, influential and history-making individuals are the ones who crushed their fears and jumped out on the path to attainment.

How to Crush Fear

Success leaves clues. And the way to banish fear is the way all achievers have done. By facing the fear and moving forward anyway. Emerson once said, "do the thing you fear and the death of fear is certain." Truer words were never spoken.

Do the thing you fear and the death of fear is certain. Face it, stare it down and it will shrink like a coward. Fears may never leave us but we can overcome them and in doing so - we diminish their hold and power over us.

Two keys to help in this battle are visualization and affirmation. Both principles are very effective in fighting fear and his twin brother, doubt.

If there is a goal you want to reach or a phobia (fear of snakes, heights, etc.) that needs banished - visualize the end result. See yourself overcoming the fear (phobia) and reaching the goal. If you do this enough and on a regular basis - results will show up in your life.

My personal favorite is affirmation. And the best is a simple three-word phrase I've used every time I suffer fear and doubt going after my goals. The simple phrase is: Do It Now!

Trust me on this. I read 'Success Through a Positive Mental Attitude,' by W. Clement Stone and Napoleon Hill many, many years ago and that's where I learned the do it now technique. It works 100 percent of the time - if you try it.

Write the words in big block letters on an index card and keep them with you always. When you're going for your goals and fear and doubt show up, say over and repeatedly: Do it Now! Do It Now! You'll be amazed at how much you can accomplish. I guarantee it.

Fear is a learned response. Don't let it keep you from achieving your dreams. Use visualization and affirmations to change your belief system and crush fear forever. Demand the impossible, dream your destiny and go after your goals with a fearless heart.

DO IT NOW!

How to Destroy Procrastination

The single biggest problem keeping people from reaching a high level of success, besides not having a definite purpose, is that good old enemy known as procrastination.

Putting things off indefinitely that should be done now is an all-too common problem in society today. In the 21st century, personal computers, cell phones, PDA's, laptops, mp3 players, video games and 500-channel satellite television provide a ready made source of distraction more so than in any other time in history.

Indecision and withering imaginations are commonplace occurrences in the pop culture of today. Unfortunately, all this mental stimulation or as I like to say, mental medication, has left many individuals without definite goals, plans to achieve them or the ability to begin a seemingly difficult task in the first place.

Even with all this mental noise around us, there is a way to break it's spell. The way to end procrastination is actually easy. Whenever you're faced with a decision, instead of putting it off till later, DO IT NOW!

Those three little magic words can help spur you on to unimaginable levels of achievement. The Nike slogan, 'Just Do It' is appropriate as well. When you feel like procrastinating say to yourself, do it now or just do it and take immediate action from where you stand.

If you follow this simple rule of saying do it now over and over and then take action, it won't be long until procrastination is a thing of the past in your life. Procrastination dies when presented with any action and repeated affirmations of action words will allow you to destroy this evil villain once and for all.

The Dynamics of Motivation

Motivation is a valuable and important component to success. Without it, goals can never be accomplished. We need highly charged and emotional motivation to surmount obstacles and difficulties that will most assuredly cross our path in pursuit of a worthwhile objective.

The main questions then are, what is motivation and how can motivation be developed? Fortunately, both questions have simple, but profoundly important answers. We'll look at each one separately.

What is motivation?

The definition for motivation is pretty straight forward. **Motivation is the desire to do something based on an individual's needs or wants**

When a person has a need or want; they will motivate themselves to perform certain functions or actions to satisfy the need or want. Needs and wants will differ from person to person, depending on individual interests, tastes and desires.

There are three categories of needs: basic, security and ego driven. Ego or self-interest needs are not needs at all, but wants. We think we need them, but actually, we don't as far as survival goes, hence the term wants.

Basic needs are just that, basic, such as food, water, shelter, clothing and air. We need these for survival. Security needs are based on safety, job security, financial stability and so on. Ego-driven wants come from the need to be loved, to find creative expression, a sense of importance and identity, and to be accepted by others.

Each individual is driven differently by the three categories of needs. My step-son Alex and his friend Aaron used to have a rock band called Recycled America. Obviously, they were motivated by the need to express themselves creatively, but every category feeds off one another. Recycled America was using the creative force of music to be accepted by others and through the music, achieve security and a sense of well being. All are working together, but the dominant need is creative expression.

Others will be driven by different needs depending on focus, goals and psychological make-up. That in a nutshell is the characteristics of motivation.

How can motivation be developed?

Motivation is developed by deciding on a goal or outcome you want to achieve and focusing on the desired outcome until it moves you to take action for its attainment. Action is the key.

If the goal is strong enough the motivation will come naturally. If you can't get up and perform the actions needed to accomplish the goal, then you don't really want it. Simple as that and no amount of visualization or self-talk will help you.

Life is based on action. Movement creates a result. Like we were taught in high school physics: **every action has an equal or opposite reaction**. Life is movement. The greatest idea in the world is nothing until you take action on it. Then and only then, does it become reality.

Pick a goal that inspires and lights a fire in your soul, focus on its attainment without distractions, smash obstacles that stand in the way, and take action to make your vision a reality. Make no mistake, action can precede motivation. If you aren't feeling motivated, take fresh action and the motivation will come.

Follow those simple steps and motivation will be as natural to you as breathing. That is the dynamics of motivation.

Nothing happens without movement and nothing will happen in your life if you don't follow the third pillar of success – take **action!**

Seize the Day!

People are judged by what they think and what they say. But the true measure of their character is what they **do**. Anyone who has achieved success and fortune in the world has done it by action.

William Jennings Bryan wrote, *"Destiny is not a matter of chance, it is a matter of choice; it is not a thing to be waited for, it is a thing to be achieved."*

The choice of the path you follow is often put before you as opportunity. *"Few people recognize opportunity"* said Thomas Edison, *"because it comes disguised as hard work."*

Don't let opportunities slip past while you're still considering them, and create new ones as you see them. *"Wise people make more opportunities than they find",* said Francis Bacon.

What opportunities can you act upon?

- ✓ Woolworth saw a need for small inexpensive items and opened a chain of stores that grossed billions.

- ✓ Wrigley started giving gum away as a bonus from a supplies wagon he sold from, and saw the opportunity to make money from the gum that became in high demand.

All successful people the world over have found the opportunities for their own special talents and acted upon those ways to achieve. *Why wait* for the time to pass?

There will never a better time than now- for you days are numbered and you know not your final breath.

Lewis Carroll believed as many as **six impossible things** before breakfast. Take your own impossible dreams and make them reality.

PILLAR FOUR:
Persistence

"Perseverance is the single most important quality needed to succeed."

John D. Rockefeller

No matter how positive an attitude you have, how hard you work and how good you are at what you do, there will be times when problems arise. In those times when it seems like Murphy's Law is hitting you smack dab in the face, you need to have an abundance of perseverance.

Never quitting, never giving up, good old perseverance is a character trait all successful people have. No matter what you consider a success, stick-to-it-iv-ness is essential to achieving your goals.

Edison was fond of saying many people quit, give up, when success is right within their grasp. How sad and how true the statement really is. Too many individuals give up at the first sign of trouble.

Obstacles and problems are put in your path for you to learn from and grow in strength. If you quit then you set up in your mind a failure mentality that can drag you down for the rest of your life. A repeated pattern of giving up sets up neuron connections in your brain that creates a quitting response whenever setbacks arise.

This bad habit, like all habits can be broken. What one needs to do is anytime a setback, problem or obstacle arises, look for the benefit and the good it can teach you.

Resolve to never quit, to keep on going. Work your way around, through or under the obstacle. A repeated pattern of looking for the lessons and finding a solution to any problem creates a new set of neuron connections, which will allow you to keep charging ahead until the goal is reached.

Perseverance is a key ingredient in the recipe of success. Make no mistake, problems will arise, obstacles will block your path. This is just a test to set you on the right way and see if you really want what you say you want.

If you hang in there and resist the urge to quit, success is practically assured. Remember the famous words of Winston Churchill, "never, never, never quit."

How Good is Your Lemonade?

One of the biggest differences on the thin line between success and failure is the habit of finding the good hidden in the bad. It's a habit that separates winners from losers.

Taking adversity and turning it into an advantage is an art. On the bright side, it is a learned art. All it takes is practice and consistency.

Life is going to throw you curveballs. It doesn't matter how much money, power, or fame you have. Troubles come and nothing on earth can stop them. The key is to take those troubles and search for the hidden benefit.

There's an old saying that everyone who studies success philosophy knows, "Every adversity has with it the seed of an equal or greater benefit." It's up to us to dig deep for the greater benefit and use it to propel us on our success journey.

If you want to be a success in life, you must learn to triumph over adversity. Giving up or falling into despair is not the way champions are made. That's the quitter's way. A slow decent into an unfulfilled and uninspired existence.

Problems must be overcome and obstacles smashed if one is to become a true success in life, no matter what your calling is. Overcoming difficult situations builds character and creates and undefeatable willpower that in time, will respond to your beck and call.

Adversity allows us to grow if we only train ourselves to look for the great lessons it teaches. It's all a matter of changing your focus. Concentrate on finding the benefit instead of obsessing on all the wrong things. Do this and problems will be discarded from your life like an old shirt no longer useful.

"When life gives you lemons, make lemonade," has been the slogan for many a success in all fields and areas of life.

Thomas J. Watson (IBM), Charles Revson (Revlon), George Eastman (Kodak), Andrew Carnegie (U.S. Steel), Henry Ford (Ford Motor Company) and Larry Ellison (Oracle) were all high school dropouts. Other business leaders such as Bill Gates (Microsoft), Michael Dell (Dell Computers) and John D. Rockefeller (Standard Oil) didn't complete college. A lack of education didn't stop them from becoming titans in the business world.

Einstein and Edison were both called idiots who would be nothing but failures by their grammar school teachers. How wrong they were. History has proven it. Edison is the greatest inventor of all-time and Einstein its greatest physicist.

There are so many examples we could go on all day. Suffice it to say life will give you what you want provided one has a definite goal, belief in its achievement, takes action and learns to see the hidden good in all obstacles and problems.

How good is your lemonade? It all depends on your own perceptions.

Have You've Been Rejected? That's Great!

Rejection is not the end; it's a starting point to something greater coming in your life. But only if you realize it and look for the benefit in this life lesson.

Far too many want to roll into a ball, assume the fetal position and give up when rejection hits them. Some sadly give up and never take any risk or make any important decisions for the rest of their lives. They close up shop on their dreams and become content to exist, instead of really living.

All because of rejection, fear and self doubt. How silly. It doesn't have to be that way at all. In fact, rejection and defeat can be one of the best things to happen to you.

Why? It's simple really. Rejection is someone else's opinion. That's all, nothing more. And no one should have so much power over you. If they do, stop it right now! You were made to succeed. Rejection is foolish to even respond or react to.

The opinions of others have no hold on you. All they can do is hurt your feelings, not your success. Only you can hurt your success by giving up and quitting. Only if you listen and believe in what they say can you be stopped short of the goal.

Usually when someone's rejected it means success is just around the corner. Just believe and persist.

Sylvester Stallone took his script to 39 movie producers and was rejected by 38 of those. The 39th said yes he'd make the movie. 'Rocky' became a phenomenon and made Sly a very rich man.

Edison tried 1,000 different experiments in creating the light bulb and finally succeeded on number 1,001. He was ridiculed and laughed at in public but he strove on.

While still a boy, Pete Gray lost his right arm in an automobile accident. His dream was to be a major league baseball player and now here he was, without his dominant arm trying to play a game that's difficult for people without a handicap. Most would have given up and wallowed in resentment and self-pity.

Not Gray. Even as a boy, he had the mental makeup of a champion. He was determined to be a professional baseball player and nothing would stand in his way. When you have persistence like this, when only the goal and nothing else is in sight, obstacles will crumble before you. Here's the rest of his amazing story.

The naturally right-handed youngster learned to throw and bat from the opposite side. Batting with one arm, Gray sprayed line drives around the field. On the base paths, he displayed speed and daring, and fielding was a study in agility and dexterity.

After catching a fly ball, Gray would tuck his thinly padded glove under his stump; roll the ball across his chest, and throw, all in one fluid motion.

Gray was a semi-pro star in the coal towns of his native Pennsylvania and with the famed Brooklyn Bushwicks. He entered pro ball in 1942 with Three Rivers (Canadian-American League) and hit .381 in 42 games. In the Southern Association in 1943, Gray hit .289 in a full season with Memphis.

He won national attention in 1944 when he batted .333 for Memphis, hit five HR, tied a league record by stealing 68 bases, and was named the Southern Association's MVP.

This outstanding showing earned Gray a spot with the 1945 St. Louis Browns. He had done what many thought impossible – Pete Gray became a major leaguer.

These are just some examples of many that show persistence in the face of rejection. Ignore the criticism, cast it aside. The only opinion that matters is the one you hold of yourself.

Rejection has no power over you. Learn from the rejection, take what it teaches and focus on bigger things than the opinions of others - namely your future success.

Become so obsessed with your goal that the sting of rejection cannot penetrate your mind. Think only of achievement and accomplishment, never of quitting or failure. Use the incredible power of your mind to overcome rejection and all obstacles that stand in your way.

And when you learn to do that - success will be waiting to great you with open arms.

Defeat Resistance with Persistence

Excuse me for the bad alliteration, but it sounded pretty cool and makes an even better point.

Resistance, adversity and troubles will come to us. It's inevitable, a fact of life. As long as you are breathing in H_2O and breathing out CO_2, there will be certain times in your existence that just plain suck.

It's how you deal with those periods of intense suckiness that matter the most. Unfortunately, many choose the worst method of all - ignore the problem and hope it will eventually go away. C'mon people, you know it doesn't work. Ignoring a problem always comes back to bite you.

Still others curl up into a ball and practice with perfection the woe-is-me self-pity that drives family and friends crazy. Others take their problem or God forbid, problems, to said friends and family and pray they deal with it. This one is especially true if it's a money problem.

In all those examples one thing is common - the problem or the resistance the individual is facing controls them and not the other way around. The only way to conquer adversity, resistance or a particular problem is to stand up to it, plan a way to overcome it and follow the plan with steel resolve until the desired outcome has transpired.

Adversity shrinks away a coward when a person is endowed with unconquerable persistence. This type of persistent effort mows down all opposition and roots out any obstacle standing in the way. The good news is it can be developed. Persistence doesn't discriminate. The wealthy can't lay claim to it at the expense of everyone else. Genetics play no part. It's a spiritual principle that's undeniable and open to the world.

The key to harnessing this power of unwavering persistence is to create a vision. Picture the life you want to have, create a plan to make it happen, take action and live in that mental picture until the desired outcome comes about. Never take your eyes off the goal. Stay focused and don't get distracted from what you want.

If it's a particular problem you're facing, like lack of funds to pay bills, immediately take your focus off the negative, and concentrate on the solution and the life you've planned. I know this can be difficult, but the process must be consistently practiced in order to conquer your adversity. Run different scenarios around and see what may or may not work.

When a solution appears, which it will if you practice this technique, take action immediately until the problem is solved. Persistence can be mastered, but you must work at it.

Therefore, when you're faced with a problem or resistance of any kind, take your thoughts off the problem and focus on the solution. Concentrate on the ideal life you're creating, take action to make it a reality and never, ever give up.

Do this and you not only master the fourth pillar of success - **persistence**. You'll master yourself as well.

"Nothing in this world can take the place of persistence. Talent will not; nothing is more common than unsuccessful people with talent. Genius will not; unrewarded genius is almost a proverb. Education will not; the world is full of educated derelicts. Persistence and determination alone are omnipotent. The slogan "press on" has solved and always will solve the problems of the human race."

Calvin Coolidge

Chapter 5:
Gratitude & Giving

If you knew what I know about the power of giving, you would not let a single meal pass without sharing it in some way.

Buddha

This will come as a shock to you. Some may have read or heard something similar before and either ignored it, didn't believe or just forgot about it.

Just like all secrets to a successful life are not really secret. It is a fundamental principle of an abundant life that has gone unnoticed, unheeded or forgotten.

This principle, coupled with faith and action, is the foundation of having anything your heart desires. Obey it and the keys to open the gates of achievement are yours.

World religions have spoken and taught the value of its practice from generation to generation. Yet, ironically, this timeless wisdom has been unused and discarded by the majority.

Some through ignorance, some from lack of understanding and others because of sheer selfishness.

Many success or self-improvement writers have failed to bring this principle out of the darkness and into the light again. Therefore, this awesome law of abundance has remained hidden, waiting to be re-discovered.

 What is this amazing principle, this law of abundance that will give you anything you want in life? What is this powerful, all encompassing universal law?

The answer my friend is deceptively simple. It's the law of giving, the principle of sowing and reaping. Also known as the law of reciprocity or the Golden Rule – do unto others as you would have done unto you.

If you want anything in life in abundance, you must give it away. Do you want more money? Give some to others. Do you want more friends? Become friendlier. Do you want love? Start giving away the love inside you.

If you hoard what you have, the universe will keep its gifts from you. Sowing and reaping - cause and effect. Even if you're not a religious person and have no belief in God, this principle still applies. Look around, open your eyes and see, the law is everywhere working its magic.

Relationships come about when two people decide to share souls with each other. To earn a living you have to deliver a certain service and in turn, your employer gives you money. If you have your own business and can't serve (give) properly, you'll be looking for a j-o-b in no time.

All progress is give and take, sowing and reaping. If people wouldn't invest or give of their time, money and talents, then life as we know it would cease to be. Hoarding and selfishness is against nature. The rain gives of itself and causes the grass, trees, plants and flowers to grow.

 In turn, they give shelter, food and joy to man and animal alike.

It's the reason we have what we have today. Without giving and receiving, man would still be living in caves, afraid and creating for himself a meaningless existence.

In order to receive the benefits of this timeless principle- just start practicing it. That's all there is to it. Give and you shall receive. It cannot fail to reproduce after its kind. You must be a cheerful giver and a cheerful receiver for it to work magic in your life. If you complain after you give or feel guilty for receiving, you are diminishing its power.

Do you want abundance, love, harmonious relationships, a successful career and all that this world has to offer?

Start giving with joy and faith and watch the amazing things that happen in your life.

The Attitude of Gratitude/The Law of Service

There is one great all-embracing Law, which is the foundation and cause of the universe, the Law of Love. It has been called by many names in various countries and at various times, but behind all its names the eye of Truth may discover the same unalterable Law.

Names, religions, personalities pass away, but the Law of Love remains. To become possessed of knowledge of this Law, to enter into conscious harmony with it, is to become immortal, invincible, and indestructible.

The Law is impersonal, and its highest manifested expression is that of Service.

The glory alike of the saint, the sage, and the savior is this - that he has realized the most profound lowliness, the most sublime unselfishness; having given up all, even his own personality, all his works are holy and enduring, for they are freed from every taint of self.

He gives, yet never thinks of receiving; he works without regretting the past or anticipating the future, and never looks for reward.

When the farmer has tilled and dressed his land and put in the seed, he knows he has done all he can possibly do, and now he must trust to the elements, and wait patiently for the course of time to bring about the harvest, and no amount of expectancy on his part will affect the result.

Even so, he who has realized Truth goes forth as a sower of the seeds of goodness, purity, love and peace, without expectancy, and never looking for results, knowing there is the Great Over-ruling Law, which brings about its own harvest in due time, and which is alike the source of preservation and destruction.

What the saints, sages, and saviors have accomplished, you likewise may accomplish if you will only tread the same path and pointed out, the way of self-sacrifice, of self-denying service.

Whoever fights ceaselessly against his own selfishness, and strives to supplant it with all-embracing love, is a saint, whether he lives in a hovel or in the midst of riches and influence; or whether he preaches or remains obscure.

And this only is true service – to forget oneself in love towards all, to lose oneself in working for the whole.

It is given to the world to learn one great and divine lesson, the lesson of absolute unselfishness.

 All the Scriptures of the world are framed to teach this one lesson; all the great teachers reiterate it. It is too simple for the world which, scorning it, stumbles along in the complex ways of selfishness.

We must have a humble heart and strive with all our might to help others along the path of life. For if we do, the rewards will be great.

Life is giving and you must give to live. It is a known spiritual law – not by hoarding do you come into abundance but by freely giving what you have – for as you sow, so shall you reap.

And when you give of your time, or money or service, perform it with an attitude of gratitude. If you give expecting something in return or with a begrudging or selfish heart – the universe cannot or will not – give back to you in kind.

Gratitude does not need explanation - you know how to be grateful. But did you know gratitude brings you more of what you appreciate? Gratitude speeds along the manifestation of your desires.

When you find things you appreciate and you use them as your point of focus, your world has to get better in every area of your life.

Look around you right now. What can you be grateful for? Make a list. Get into the authentic feeling of true gratitude.

Find something, anything, to be grateful for right now. When you are grateful, you're in a high-energy vibration that will attract more things to be grateful for and more good things will come to you magically, drawn in by your feelings of gratitude.

Every morning when you first get up and every evening before going to bed, make a list of all the things you are grateful for. Doing this opens the floodgates to all that is possible in the universe.

What the Bible Says About Success

While most people believe the pursuit of success is a modern day obsession, nothing could be further from the truth. Down through the ages, ambitious men and women pursued lofty goals and aspirations with the hope of achieving financial and physical comforts.

Even the Bible spelled out detailed advice for those wishing to pursue their dreams and goals. It is these success principles I would like to focus on.

Without a doubt, the most significant verse in the Bible pertaining to achieving success is found in the Gospel of Mark. In Mark 9:23 of the KJV its states, "If thou canst believe, all things are possible to him who believes."

If you develop the kind of belief or faith the Bible describes as Jesus taught, nothing would be impossible for you. NOTHING!!! How unbelievable and inspiring is that.

A similar passage is related in Matthew 17:20, when Jesus said, "If ye have faith (belief) as a grain of mustard seed, ye shall say to this mountain (obstacle), remove hence to yonder place and it shall remove, and nothing shall be impossible unto you."

Belief is the cornerstone to success; doubt and fear are the cripplers of achievement. You will find this truth in James 1:5-6. "But let him ask in faith, nothing wavering. For he that wavereth is like a wave of the sea driven with the wind and tossed."

Focused work in your chosen field is also an essential ingredient for success. In Proverbs 22:29 we read, "Seest thou a man diligent in his business? He shall stand before kings; he shall not stand before mean men."

Laziness or half-hearted effort will lead to disaster. In Proverbs 6:9-11 it spells this out very clearly. "How long wilt thou sleep, O sluggard? When wilt thou arise out of thy sleep? Yet a little sleep, a little slumber, a little folding of the hands to sleep: So shall thy poverty come as one that travelleth, and thy want as an armed man."

Finally, we have a success principle in Hebrews that wasn't understood until now, thanks to the advancement of Quantum Mechanics and the field of Neuroscience.

In Hebrews 11:3, we have the very profound statement, "Through faith we understand that the worlds were framed by the word of God, so that things which are seen were not made of things which do appear." It's the last part of the verse you need to focus on.

Things, which are seen, were made by things we cannot see, the invisible quantum world. Through our visualization and persistent thought, we create the fabric of our lives. Joined with faith, laser-like focus, and action, you have an unstoppable combination for success in any endeavor.

Now whether you believe in God or not is your own personal decision, but even if you don't, apply these principles and use their teachings for your own pursuit of a successful life.

Look Deep Within

Not all success can be counted in dollars; not all richness is measured by money.

"The great secret of success is to go through life as a person who never gets used up," said Albert Schweitzer.

Look within yourself for the ultimate inspiration, and follow the true feelings you discover. *"One of my favorite methods is to whisper,"* said Alfred Hitchcock. *"I've discovered the best work is done with sweet reason."*

Act upon your own conscience -that guides; that judges your actions and signals your behavior. *"Conscience is the inner voice that warns us that someone may be looking,"* wrote H.L. Mencken.

Accomplish what you desire; fulfill your inner yearnings. But don't compromise your deepest feelings.

"We do our best that we know how at the moment, and if it doesn't turn out, we modify it," said Franklin Delano Roosevelt.

Follow the paths life offers you and live the fullest existence you can.

Look at yourself and at those who have succeeded throughout history. Do you have what it takes? Even if you have only a few of these qualities, you can achieve your heart's desire.

Reach for the highest, *and then reach higher.*

Accomplish your steps one by one on a **daily** basis, always moving forward, always making progress, even if only "part and parcel". Encourage yourself.

Insist you can succeed and affirm these thoughts daily.

Keep a sense of proportion and judge for yourself. Then keep busy at the tasks you've set out to accomplish. What's keeping you?

"Genius is one percent inspiration and ninety-nine percent perspiration," said Albert Einstein.

Find inspiration wherever you can. Talk to people; read about people; learn your business or craft. Believe you can do it and you will. The only way to dispel the doubt you can do something is to **finish it**.

Always be the best you can be.

Never fall short from fatigue or lethargy.

Don't attempt to do anything you can't give your all to.

There is no way to inner satisfaction without appealing to the higher self/ consciousness.

Search within and without to find the paths meant for you and follow them with conviction and a steady heart.

And, you will succeed to become as rich and full as you ever desired.

Harold Ickes wanted the *"freedom to live one's life with the window of the soul, open to new thoughts, new ideas and new aspirations."*

In addition, Woody Allen looked for a clear path. *"If only God would give me some clear sign,"* he said. *"Like making a large deposit in my name at a Swiss bank."*

Finally, Sophie Tucker sums up everyone's worldly outlook: *"I've been rich and I've been poor,"* she said. *"Rich is better."*

Chapter 6: Good Health

To get rich never risk your health. For it is the truth that health is the wealth of wealth.

Richard Baker

Without good health, all achievement would be empty and meaningless. What good is it to accomplish all your goals if you can't enjoy the fruits of your efforts?

Sickness and disease can and shouldn't be a part of our lives. Ill health is not part of our natural condition. We were made to be strong, energetic and vital.

Sickness falls on us when we violate the natural laws of good health.

Excessive smoking, alcohol consumption, drug abuse and high fat foods break down the natural immune system and leave us broken and vulnerable to sickness and disease.

What's worse is we know these toxic substances and bad diet can cause the very sickness we want to avoid, but continue to abuse ourselves anyway.

And while it is not the intention of this author to pretend to be an expert in health or nutrition, I do feel that enough information about proper exercise and diet is out there to comment on.

Healthy Living: The Key to Successful Living

Let's face it - without healthy living, we can't possibly have successful living. Good health is the single most important component to a successful life.

With it, you can enjoy the fruits this world has to offer. Without it, all the money in the world is meaningless.

Good health isn't just about eating right. There are more components involved in the health equation than just eating your fruits and veggies, whole grains and lean proteins.

Although good eating habits are a start, we must incorporate exercise, sufficient sleep, quality relationships and proper mental and emotional attitudes to complete the total health picture.

If any of these five key factors are missing from our lives, we cannot possibly be at our best and most efficient. In order to have a more clear-cut picture in mind of what total health is, we need to break down the five key factors of good health one-by-one.

Nutrition

Probably no topic, with the exception of religion and politics, has as much debate, controversy and disagreement surrounding it than nutrition.

From Atkins to South Beach, from low-carb to high-carb and every fad diet in-between - from celebrities, PhD holders, gym owners, to the guy down the street. All have an opinion on proper diet and healthy nutrition.

And while this author is not a nutrition expert or a doctor, I say it's time for a little intelligence and common sense to take over and settle the argument once and for all.

Common sense tells us all a proper diet is one that contains lots of fruits, veggies, some whole grains (after exercise), and lean protein (chicken, fish, beef) with some healthy fats (nuts, olive oil) thrown in for good measure. Also, don't forget to drink plenty of water and get some daily dairy as well.

Common sense also tells us processed foods high in saturated and trans fats are a no-no. These include chips, processed sugary treats, fast food and anything made with white flour. Now this doesn't mean you have to become monk-like and completely abstain from these foods - just eat them sparingly. I like a good brownie every now and then, just not every day. If you like fast food, go out once or twice a month and treat yourself. Be sensible with your eating habits and patterns.

Deprivation and diets do not work. The perfect balance is to eat healthy 90 percent of the time and with the other 10 percent - eat what you want, just eat it sparingly. Have a cheat day like pro athletes and bodybuilders do.

Life is supposed to be savored and enjoyed. If you're constantly getting down on yourself for eating a doughnut or whatever, that's not healthy either. Relax, eat the doughnut if you want, but eat only one and not on a regular basis and you'll be fine. Stop beating yourself up over it.

We can go too far on the supposed healthy side as well. Take for instance the no-carb craze. Some take it to such extremes they won't even eat a piece of fruit, because the fructose is too high in carbohydrates. Give me a break!

No one and I mean no one, is going to tell or convince me fruits are bad. They come from nature, were put here by God and they're supposed to be our true candy. The sweetness in fruit is nature's gift to us - not a Milky Way or Snickers. Fruit is good. Besides, the body needs carbohydrates for energy. The brain itself feeds off one thing and one thing only - carbs. The low carb people need to get a grip. It's empty carb foods like chips and cookies that are bad, not a grape.

The final problem in the nutrition debate is eating frequency. We here in America eat too damned much. I don't care if you follow a very clean, healthy diet - eating too much and too frequently hurts the digestive system by not giving it a chance to relax and take a break. I'm not a doctor, but I have experience on this eating too much stuff, just ask my acid-reflux filled stomach if the digestive system needs a break or not.

Eating the five, six or seven meals a day some recommend is ridiculous. We need to eat less not more. Numerous studies have proven that calorie restriction is a known factor in extending life expectancy.

Two to four meals per day is all anyone really needs for energy, health and proper nutrition. The majority who don't exercise should eat 2-3 meals, while the exercisers should go with four, since they're using up more energy on a daily basis.

Fasting is another integral part of a complete, healthy nutrition plan. Fasting isn't just for religious purposes. Fasting cleans the body of impurities and stimulates the mind to creative thought and ideas. Everyone should fast on a weekly basis, either through intermittent fasting or a 24-hour fast once or twice a week.

Finally, don't forget to take a multi-vitamin daily. No one eats right all the time, so a vitamin is a good insurance policy.

So here in a nutshell, using only the tools of intelligence and common sense, we have come up with a complete, easy to follow nutrition plan for good health.

1. Eat fruits and veggies daily.
2. Eat whole grains daily (only after exercise).
3. Eat some healthy fats (Olive Oil, nuts) daily.
4. Drink plenty of water every day.
5. Eat some lean protein (fish, chicken, lean beef) daily.
6. Don't forget your dairy.
7. Eat 2-4 meals per day.
8. Fast once a weak or use intermittent fast daily (16 hour fast)
9. Take a multi-vitamin daily.
10. Treat yourself to some junk food if you want, only do so sparingly on cheat days.

Follow the above ten steps and you don't need to buy another diet book ever again…unless you want to.

Exercise

Nothing has more of a profound, positive benefit on the body than exercise, even more so than nutrition.

Exercise is the single best thing a person can do to improve health and keep diseases at a distance. Physical exercise is not just for weight control purposes. The benefits of regular aerobic and anaerobic (weight lifting) exercise are numerous.

Exercise has many benefits:

1. Improves health and longevity.
2. Prevents heart disease by lowering cholesterol and high blood pressure.
3. Helps prevent certain types of cancers.
4. Keeps type-II diabetes at bay.
5. Helps prevent arthritis and improves bone density, which prevents osteoporosis.
6. Improves mood.
7. Controls weight by speeding up the metabolism and increasing muscle.

That increased lean muscle mass leads to greater fat burning and insulin control - resulting in normal weight levels.

Without exercise, our muscles atrophy and waste away. In time, this muscle wasting will cause an individual to gain more fat and have less energy - leaving one open to diabetes, heart disease and stroke.

As you can see, exercise is a major component, if not the most important one, in living a healthy and successful life.

New findings have shown we do not need marathon exercise sessions lasting hours and hours. In fact, too much exercise, such as the workout regimens of long-distance runners, can cause serious health problems as well.

It's called the overtraining principle and it occurs when excessive amounts of exercise cause too much stress on the body with not enough recovery time given to re-energize and repair the body.

The key to quality exercise is the intensity of aerobic workouts performed and the addition of weight training to anyone's healthy living program.

Aerobic Exercise

Japanese scientist Izumi Tabata found that shorter, more vigorous exercise had greater cardiovascular and anaerobic benefits than longer steady-state type workouts.

Tabata Intervals consist of 20 seconds of flat out effort followed by 10 seconds of rest for eight intervals. Add a four-minute warm-up with a four-minute cool-down and you have a grand total of only a 12-minute workout.

The problem is they're not easy and should only be performed if you're already in decent shape. Beginners can perform brisk walking or stationary cycling without the intervals until they are in better shape. After a period of time, intervals can and should be added to any aerobic program.

Here is a sample program that anyone who is new to exercise or out of shape can follow:

Walk, bike, jog or use any aerobic apparatus (stationary cycle, versa climber, rowing machine) 20-30 minutes at a time, 3-4 days per week.

After about six months, add in some Tabata Intervals slowly until you've reached the 12-minute protocol (four-minute warm-up, four-minute intervals, four-minute cool down).

Weight Training

Weight training should be performed 2-3 days per week consisting of major compound exercises that work the overall musculature of the body.

Lifting weights is the best exercise in the world and should be incorporated into everyone's exercise program. The key is progression. You must consistently lift heavier weights if you want to reap the major benefits. Remember, intensity is key.

Start out with light weights and work up as you progress and get stronger and better fit. Below is a very good beginners program. You can also use Kettlebells or your own body weight for a nice workout.

Basic Beginners Workout:

Squats 3 x 10-12
Overhead Press 3 x 8-10
Deadlifts or Shrugs 3 x 8-10
Chins or Pulldowns 3 x 8-10
Dips or Bench Press 2 x 8-10
Crunches 2 x 10-15

After you become more advanced and stronger, you'll add more weight to each exercise and drop to 1-or-2 sets per exercise. If you don't know how to perform these exercises, you can search the Internet or your local bookstore for a description of each exercise and how it should be done.

Stick with only the big exercises above. Choose the ones you like and blast them hard. Don't add any weight until you can perform all of your sets while maintaining good form. Don't forget to do some form or cardio 3-4 days per week for conditioning.

Also, give yourself at least one rest day per week where no workouts are performed. Remember, the nervous system needs to recover from exercise, so take one day off every week and just enjoy the day. Your body will thank you for the recharge.

Understand that to be successful in any weight training program - hard work is a must! Half-hearted effort does nothing for you. If you're new to weight training or grossly out of shape, please consult a physician first.

Exercise is the most important thing you can do for your body. Take it seriously because the implications are enormous.

Regular exercise combined with proper nutrition can keep illness and disease at bay and allow one to live a long, fruitful and successful life.

Eliminating Unhealthy Habits

Studies have shown that upwards of 80 percent of all heart disease and 70 percent of most cancers could be prevented if we exercised regularly, maintained a healthy diet and eliminated bad habits like smoking, drug abuse and excessive alcohol consumption.

The fact is that most diseases and sickness are caused by our habitual bad habits and if corrected, could be prevented from affecting our lives.

Making the right choices can be hard - habits are habits because they've been ingrained in our subconscious for so long we don't think about them, we just do them. Habits can seem impossible to break, but break them we must. Our lives, our health and our success are at stake if we don't snap free from the chains of our unhealthy habits.

Smoking, poor food choices, alcohol and drug abuse are the big four when it comes to causing sickness and preventable deaths in the United States. Smoking is responsible for more early deaths than any of the other unhealthy habits combined.

Heart disease, stroke and cancer victims can look to smoking as one of the main culprits. Cigarette smoking is the number one cause of premature and preventable death in the world. Smoking hardens the arteries, raises blood pressure and produces malignant cancer cells in the body.

Alcohol and drug abuse are notorious cancer causers as well as the number one cause of death by vehicle in the U.S. In addition to these, drug abusers run the risk of contracting blood born killers like AIDS and Hepatitis C.

Foods high in sugar, salt, saturated and trans fats can cause numerous damage to the body. Most likely in the forms of heart disease, inflammation and overall ill health. Recent studies suggest that upwards of 70 percent of all deaths in the United States can be attributed to these four deadly habits.

Breaking the Cycle

These habits, especially smoking, are so powerful many people even after suffering debilitating health problems will not stop their unhealthy habit. The point is the habit can become a very potent addiction over time.

Fortunately, there are ways to break bad habits and addictions for good. Here are six steps to getting free from any unhealthy habit.

1. **Self-motivation** - before you can stop a bad habit, you must want to stop. If you can't get yourself motivated to quit, you're defeated before you start.

2. **Seek counseling or a support group** - Some may not be able to afford a counselor, but support groups can be found anywhere, including friends and family.

3. **Exercise regularly** - Nothing is more beneficial for the human body than exercise. It lowers blood pressure, cholesterol and releases endorphins (the feel good chemical) throughout the body.

4. **Reward yourself** - Set up a reward system for yourself. If you go a day without smoking, go buy yourself something; take a night out on the town or whatever rewards you can think of to keep the motivation levels high.

5. **Visualization and affirmations** - Visualize, see yourself in your mind's eye free from your bad habit or addiction. Use strong emotions to plant the vision deep in your subconscious and affirm you're free from your bad habit. It won't be long before that habit is replaced with your ideal vision.

6. **Replace a negative habit with a positive one** - This is self-explanatory. All you do is replace a bad habit (smoking) with a positive one (exercise) to take its place.

Defeating an unhealthy habit can take time, but it can be done, provided one takes persistent action and blends it with proper motivation and a solid vision of a successful outcome.

Quality Relationships

While there may be no definite evidence a loving relationship is beneficial to one's health, it certainly seems to have a positive effect on one's overall well-being.

Those who are involved in a long-term loving relationship where each person is treated with mutual respect tend to be happier, more relaxed, have more confidence and are generally healthier than individuals who don't. The reason has to do with that old bugaboo called stress. It's a well-known fact stress is a killer that can add to a host of maladies, both emotional and physical. Stress is proven to cause brain shrinkage. Stress literally kills brain cells!

If an individual is involved in a negative relationship, there is more likelihood they will suffer from stress related ailments. The more relaxed and loving a relationship is, the better the chances are that an individual will not suffer as many health problems.

Being in love and being able to share and receive affection promotes happiness, relaxation and peacefulness, which leads to less stress. Lower stress levels can lead to lower blood pressure and a much more relaxed and calm mental and emotional state of being.

People who are in abusive relationships or who live in a home environment where negativity is prevalent seem to be more susceptible to illnesses.

When suffering from stress the body's immune system may be

compromised therefore making the person more prone to flu and colds along with a host of other illnesses. Those who are involved in a stressful relationship may find themselves emotionally and physically exhausted.

A healthy relationship can improve one's well-being in a variety of ways. This is not to say a good relationship is one without disagreements or problems, but in a healthy relationship, the partners are able to talk openly and honestly with each other. They are able to work through their disagreements by having good lines of communication and are able to transcend problems that would otherwise escalate in a bad relationship.

Healthy relationships are not perfect; no relationship ever is. But when a person does not feel comfortable enough to discuss his or her feelings with a partner, those emotions will build inside, causing stress that may later lead to serious health conditions.

Whether we believe it or not, love does have a curative effect. The mind can influence the body and the healing process and when a person knows there is a stable, loving individual in their life they can depend upon, the mind is relaxed and comforted and is able to put more effort into healing the body. If a person who is in an abusive relationship becomes ill, they may not care whether they get better or not.

A quality, loving relationship is known to increase longevity. The proof is in the downward spiral of a spouse whose life-long mate passes on. We all have known someone who lost a loved one and died a short time later. A broken heart can be just as deadly as a diseased one.

Loving, healthy relationships are an important ingredient to success. Just look at history and see how many individuals were spurred on to greatness after finding the love of their life. Positive energy directed at any object will eventually cause great things to happen. Such is the power of love directed at the object of your desire.

Yes, you can achieve success without the love of a soul mate, but it's much more difficult and a much more empty process. Love is the elixir for our soul, the tonic that heals all ills. Cultivate love; not only for your family, but also for everyone you meet. In the end, beauty fades, money comes and goes, but one thing remains constant - love.

And as the Bible so eloquently states: "Love hopes all things, bears all things, believes all things. Love never ends."

Positive Mental Attitudes

Happiness is an important key, maybe the most important, to having a long life. People who suffer from depression, anxiety and stress often age quickly and die prematurely as numerous studies have shown.

A positive mental attitude has been shown in some scientific studies to have a greater affect on longevity and health than being obese, smoking or drinking.

And while nobody can be totally positive and upbeat all the time, those who are predominantly in that optimistic frame of mind tend to live longer, become more successful, are happier and more fulfilled than those who don't.

Everything starts in the mind. Every technological advancement, every successful business, anything that's ever been made was first an idea - a thought held in the mind. It only makes sense that if you want to have good health and a positive outlook on life, you must first create in your mind the conditions for health and optimism.

It's a simple process that's sometimes hard to do. Partly because of fear and doubt and partly through a lack of understanding of the mind and its power. If you want to be positive, think and act in a positive way. If you want to be healthy, think thoughts of health and vitality and as you think, so shall you be.

Emerson said, "The ancestor of every action is a thought." If you think healthy, positive thoughts, consistently holding them in the mind, you'll eventually take the actions necessary to make your thoughts reality. Think, do and become is the process.

Love is an important component in the quest for good health and in developing a positive frame of mind.

Satisfaction in a loving relationship is more conducive to good health and a positive outlook than money, job, sex or social status.

In the Bible, God says faith, hope and love last forever, but the greatest of these is love. A life filled with love is more powerful than any force in the universe. All things are possible with love. Cultivate it, nurture it and let it grow and you'll be unstoppable.

Another important factor in the happiness quotient is to take hold of the present moment and live it to the fullest. Human beings suffer from a disease I like to call the Comparison Syndrome.

We waste so much of our precious time either comparing our life to others, having flashbacks of the past to what we think were better days or looking ahead to the future and how life will be different and better. When we do this, we miss living in the only piece of time at our disposal - the ever-present now.

Now is all we have people. Nothing else is guaranteed us. Our time on Earth is a speck, a flickering flame on an almost burned out candle. So why spend it in a constant state of worry, depression and anxiety? These conditions do nothing but make us feel worse and quicken the time we do have.

Don't compare yourself to others. Each one of us is unique. We all have special skills and qualities and it's up to us to find what they are and pursue our chosen destiny.

Life is meant to be lived, savored and enjoyed. In the end, we all end up in the same boat, so just go out and try your best, keep a positive mental attitude, set goals for yourself and take action to achieve them.

Along the way, be generous, loving and kind to others. Help people along this game of life, because we all need a helping hand at some point in our lives. Go the distance, run the race to the end. Use all your energy up until there's nothing left. Don't play it safe, life's too short for that.

Live boldly, live with passion and vigor. Like Thoreau said, "advance confidently in the direction of your dreams, endeavor to live the life that you have imagined." The best way to do that is with a positive, optimistic outlook on life.

Develop and maintain a positive mental attitude, for it can mean the difference between a life full of anger, resentment and sickness or one full of love, peace and good health.

Relax..Take it Easy

I love listening to the classic album, 'The Grand Illusion' by Styx, especially the song 'Fooling Yourself (Angry Young Man)' The beginning lines of the song always strike a chord with me.

In it, Tommy Shaw sings, "relax...take it easy" and it always gets me thinking about how many of us sabotage our lives with stress, anxiety and impatience.

The constant barrage of stimuli we face every day is causing sensory overload. We have a million and one things to do and only enough hours in the day to do a thousand of them. No wonder so many kids have ADD. If the adults have trouble coping and processing, throw in the IPods, video games and whatnot that youngsters are involved in and you begin to understand why kids have such a short attention span.

The problem with all this stress, anxiety and impatience is twofold - it's bad for our health and it cripples our ability to focus.

Without focus, we are lost. For anyone to be successful they must have concentration. Controlled focus is the ability to lock on to a task or target and keep with it until the task is completed or the target is reached. Proper focus is elimination of all distractions with single-mindedness towards a chosen goal.

There's no need for me to mention the health issue - we all know by now what stress does to the body. New studies have come out proving that high stress levels can actually cause the brain to shrink! High anxiety and stress can kill brain cells as well as wreak havoc all through the body.

This is an age of mass consumption. I want it all and I want it now is the battle cry. It's a philosophy that has no direct connection to reality, which is why we have anguish, despair, depression and people in massive amounts of debt they'll never be able to get out of.

Life doesn't work that way. Look at nature. A seed falls to the ground, in time it becomes a tree or a plant and then the cycle starts all over again.

But notice, the seed doesn't become a full-grown tree overnight. It takes years and years before it blossoms to maturity. All the secrets of life are in that tree. Learn its lessons and become wiser for it.

Plant your seeds (your goals), watch over them (focus), care for them (action) and in due time, with due diligence - the completed goals are materialized and accomplished.

Stress and anxiety breed impatience. Impatience causes lack of focus and that in turn causes indecision. Indecision leads to even more stress and anxiety, which of course can grow into fear, doubt and depression.

Learn to prioritize. Make a list of the important tasks of the day. If it's not on the list - don't do it. If it is, don't let the day fade away without completing it. Many of us waste our time on trivial matters, while more important areas of our lives suffer neglect. Don't let this happen to you.

Decide on a course and stay with it. Know in your heart what you truly desire is coming to you and be patient for its arrival. You desires will come, but in their own sweet time. Just keep focusing on what you want and take continuous action to make it happen. Learn patience. If you're impatient and want it too soon, if you try too hard to grasp for the brass ring - you may fall and lose it all.

Deep down in our souls, we know what's important and what isn't. Spending time with loved ones - important. Spending time watching TV and ignoring our loved ones - not important.

Focusing on areas that can make you more successful - important. Spending your time reading the latest celebrity gossip - not important.

It's easy to prioritize once you're focused. Keep your mind on the things you want and off the things you don't want.

You can't possibly be at your best when under stress, so take some solid advice from a classic rock song - "relax...take it easy." And watch what a difference it can make in your life.

Chapter 7: Putting It All Together

"Whatever course you decide upon, there is always someone to tell you that you are wrong. There are always difficulties arising, which tempt you to believe that your critics are right. To map out a course of action and follow it to an end requires courage."

Ralph Waldo Emerson

Six Tips for a More Productive Day

Anxiousness and stress are all too common conditions in this modern world of ours. Trying to squeeze the demands of living in this fast-paced society into 24 hours and being productive to boot seems an impossibility.

Many long for simpler times when people and events moved at a much slower pace. Life was quiet and more relaxed. Well, unless you decide to buy your own deserted island or shut yourself off from the world - the simple life is out of the question. Mass communication has put an end to that.

Don't get discouraged. There are ways to take control of your day, make it more productive, joyful, fun, and relatively stress free all at the same time. All it takes is the willingness to take control of your life and follow a few simple steps.

Most of these tips you'll know and probably have heard them before. That's because they work. All you have to do is be determined to apply them every day until you have control over your own life.

Six Tips For a More Productive Day

1. **Create and write out a plan each and every day** - In order to get what you want, you have to know where you're going. Don't drift. Plan your day each and every day. It doesn't have to be elaborate. A to-do list on scrap paper is good for the task. This gives direction and purpose in your life. Don't forget to plan your day.

2. **Prioritize your day** - Take your to-do list for the day and prioritize it. Your most important tasks of the day should be put at the top and done first before anything else.

3. **Always focus on one task at a time** - Lack of concentration

is a major reason why many people have trouble getting things done. In order to have a more productive day, focus all your energies on one task at a time. Put that type of concentration into your daily tasks and you'll accomplish more in one month than some people do in a year.

4. **Live in the now** - Don't dwell in the past or live in the future. That's unproductive. All we have and all we are is in the now. Learn to keep your thoughts in the now and all the beauty and wonder this life has will unfold before your eyes.

5. **Practice gratitude and giving** - Giving of yourself and living with a persistent gratitude will work wonders in your life. Being truly thankful for what you have and what you are is the first step in vanquishing self-doubt, fear and lack. Giving and being grateful engulf your spirit with such joy that stress and anxiousness have no reason to stay in your life.

6. **Make time for solitude** - All of us need to get away from it all and have some alone time. It's a healthy and natural part of the living experience. How you use that solitude is key to being productive. Use your time for meditation, prayer or visualization. Even if think you can't be completely alone, there are ways to steal some time. Take a bath, lock yourself in your bedroom, do anything to have at least 15 minutes alone to recharge your batteries.

Stop hurrying through life anxious, stressed and unproductive. Learn to incorporate these six simple tips into your life and watch how much more productive, relaxed and in charge you really can be.

Gain Power Through Self-Development

It is the natural right of every human being to be happy. Happiness is the normal condition, as natural as the landscapes and the seasons. It is unnatural to suffer and it is only because of lack of understanding that we do suffer.

Happiness is the product of wisdom. To attain perfect wisdom, to comprehend fully the purpose of life, to realize completely the relationship of human beings to each other, is to begin climbing the ladder to wisdom and happiness. Perfect wisdom is unshadowed joy.

Why do we suffer in life? One, because of a lack of understanding of the Law of Cause and Effect and two, because we need to grow, spiritually and mentally.

By overcoming adversity, we gain in wisdom, patience and maturity. Usually we do not even see or suspect the presence of trouble until it suddenly leaps upon us like an animal in hiding.

One day our family circle is complete and happy. A week later death has come and joy is replaced with agony. Today we have a friend. Tomorrow he will be an enemy and we don't know why.

A little while ago, we had wealth and all material luxuries. There was a sudden change and now we have only poverty and misery and yet we seek in vain for a reason why this should be.

There was a time when we had health and strength; but they have both departed and no trace of a reason appears. Aside from these greater tragedies of life, innumerable things of lesser consequence continually bring to us little miseries and minor heartaches.

We most earnestly desire to avoid them but we never see them until they strike us, until in the darkness of our ignorance we blunder upon them. The thing we lack is the spiritual illumination to understand that for every cause there must be an effect. When you begin to truly understand this law, you realize that you are responsible for your own happiness or misery.

Nothing is sudden, if problems or trials have come to you; they've been stewing in your mind for some time. First thought, then action and finally, reality.

We must develop ourselves to the highest level that we can. We must always strive for the ideal of perfection, even though it doesn't exist. No one is perfect and we all have bad days from time to time, but we must work for excellence in everything we do.

In exact proportion that conscious effort is given to such self-development, only then will spiritual illumination be achieved and wisdom attained.

Thus, the light that leads to happiness is kindled from within and the evolutionary journey all are making may be robbed of its suffering.

Why do people suffer from poverty and disease? Only because we have not weeded out from our thoughts the conditions that make their existence possible, and because we do not comprehend their meaning and their lessons, nor the attitude to assume toward them.

All that's required is understanding and personal effort. When nature's lesson is fully learned these mute teachers will vanish.

Therefore, it is with all forms of suffering we experience. They are at once reactions from our ignorance and instructors that point out the better way.

When we have comprehended the lessons taught, they are no longer necessary and disappear.

It is not by the outward acquirement of facts that individuals become wise and great. It is by developing the soul from within until it illuminates our entire existence.

When we fully understand the law of cause and effect, when we harness the power of the law of action and make it our own, then and only then, will we reach true genius and leave misery and poverty to the dust of our past.

Create Your Future Right Now

The difference between those who achieve their goals and those who don't is planning and action.

Success is a science, just like biology, chemistry or geology. And just like the natural sciences, there are laws that lead to the attainment of goals. Follow them, implement them, take action and success is assured. Success is predictable. It is not based on luck or chance.

The way to success, whatever that means to you, is threefold in nature - set goals, make a plan to achieve them and take action to make them reality. Personal or financial success begins with objectives (goals). You must know what you want in order to achieve it.

Your dreams are the destinations you want to reach, your goals are the signs on the pathway to achievement. Planning is the connective tissue between your dreams, your goals and the reality of accomplishment.

So the first step on the way to creating your ideal future right now is to set goals. Once you've determined what you want the things you want have a way of finding you. Your power to achieve is based on being clear about what you want in life. If you ask for little, you get it. If you ask for the world, it's yours. As the good book says, "whatever you ask in prayer, believe that you have received it and nothing shall be impossible for you."

The best way to go about finding what you want is to play a little game of fantasy. Doesn't sound too bad does it? Imagine in your mind you had all the money, time and ability to accomplish whatever it is you want. What would it be? When you come up with the answers, which you will if you seriously try this, get out a piece of paper and start writing them down until you run out of ideas. Whatever list you have, sort them in order of importance and you have your goal list. All goals must be put to paper.

Your goals should be written down like this:

1. **Goals need to be specific and measurable** - how much

money? What color and make of car? And so on and so on.

2. **Be in the present, positive tense, stating results not wishes**- write down what the goal looks and feels like after it's accomplished. Example: Instead of writing, I will own a brand new home, state I live in a 20-acre Victorian estate with five bedrooms, three bathrooms, with lush gardens and weeping willow trees around the grounds. Make it real and in the here and now.

After your goals are written down, next you must focus on them with laser-like concentration. Your goals must become the major focus of your life if you want to attain them. Focusing on your goals leads to the development of plans by the subconscious to achieve those goals.

When the plans come, which they will if your goals are clearly the main focus of your life, take action on them immediately and eventually all your goals will bear fruit. By forming a clear mental picture of what you want and never letting go of that picture - you'll always find a way to accomplish your objectives.

Nothing happens overnight, it's not nature's way. You must commit yourself to your goals and plans and stay persistent. Remember, the larger and grander the goal, the more roadblocks you'll face. Stay persistent until the end and your dreams shall come true.

Follow the steps to creating your future right now - decide on your goals, write them down in a specific, positive, present-tense manner, focus on them until they have become your dominant thoughts and when your subconscious gives you plans to achieve your goals, take persistent, committed action until your dreams come true.

If you follow these steps to the letter. Life will give you whatever you desire.

Riches

"Had I but plenty of money, money enough to spare", wrote Robert Browning.

And money is the greatest attribute of riches. A universal desire, money is the materialization of riches, the stuff that makes the rest possible.

Are you looking for financial security?

For retirement, for education or perhaps leisure?

Riches are the **overflowing abundance** of health and wealth, which naturally includes material possessions- houses, cars, boats, furnishings...everything you ever wanted.

Centuries ago, Horace wrote, *"By right means, if you can, but by any means, make money."*

For many people it is a path towards happiness, a cure-all for worry and peace of mind. For others, riches come in the form of satisfaction and personal independence.

Satisfaction comes from accomplishment in employment or attaining goals. It is the feeling of contentment and confidence from a good task well done. Riches are closely linked with success.

And with that comes fame and acknowledgment of position. Success might be the feeling of well-being from the rewards of good effort or the enthusiasm and vitality triggered by recognition.

"Success is how well I enjoy the minutes," said producer Norman Lear. How well do you typically enjoy yours?

Throughout history, the people who lived with riches often achieved them by hard work, diligence and a belief in themselves. For some people, it took courage, genius and stamina.

But for many others, it took nothing special but the desire to turn dreams into reality.

Whether you want millions of dollars, recognition as an artist, or personal freedom, you have the ability to make your life as rich as you want.

Think about what you most desire. It may not be hard cash, but what it can buy.

Or, it may be those feelings of inner satisfaction, from creating something beautiful or strong...

Maybe personal independence from the work week, or freedom to live anywhere you want...even something meaningful and significant in life- something other than things money can buy.

Whatever your goals, and however difficult they seem to be to accomplish, you have the inherent ability to become who you want.

Take a look- can you actually *lucidly* see yourself surrounded by riches?

Picture the world open and in front of you, ready to become the form of your dreams, ready to stage your desires.

"Why then, the world's mine oyster," wrote Shakespeare, *"which I with sword will open."*

Work Towards Your Goal

"To get profit without risk, experience without danger, and reward without work, is as impossible as it is to live without being born", wrote A. P. Gouthey.

Every person who has attained something worthwhile has worked for the goal.

Cary Grant said, *"I do believe that people can do practically anything they set out to do if they apply themselves diligently and learn."*

Which path is the right way towards your goal...?

> ➤ Do you need more education?

> ➤ Do you need a few years experience in your field of business?

> ➤ Maybe you need a teacher or Mentor.

"I have learned that success is to be measured not so much by the position that one has reached, as by the obstacles which are overcome while trying to succeed", wrote Booker T. Washington.

> ➤ What obstacles are in your way?

Consider them as easy to pass through as hurdles are to a champion runner. Take each obstacle as a special challenge placed especially for you. Approach it with intelligence and courage, then learn what it has to teach.

"Success is a journey," said Ben Sweetland, *"not a destination."* For some, the process of attainment **is** the attainment itself. They move on, keep growing and expanding. There is no still water at the top.

"The message from the moon is that no problem need any longer be considered insoluble", wrote Norman Cousins. And you can attain anything that seems impossible.

If you have a problem that needs to be solved, sit calmly and consider it with a clear mind. Observe all the consequences of the actions- both good and bad.

Gently ponder the paths and actions and contemplate the core of the problem.

The solution will appear.

"Ask and it shall be given you; seek and ye shall find; knock and it shall be opened to you for everyone who asketh, receiveth. He that seeketh, findeth and to him that knocketh, it shall be opened." - Jesus of Nazareth

Tap the inner self and encourage positive actions.

With each outgoing breath, release the impossible; at each incoming breath, inhale the attainable. Command the best of yourself, but don't despair from an overused sense of perfection.

> ➢ What can you learn?

> ➢ And who can teach you?

Can you attend classes and seminars from universities near home? Check out books from the libraries and absorb the material. Find a master and become an apprentice.

"Anyone who stops learning is old, whether at twenty or eighty. Anyone who keeps learning stays young. The greatest thing in life is to keep your mind young." - Henry Ford.

Never stop learning; never stop growing and expanding as a person and in your personal endeavors.

In The End, Success is Simple

I know what you might be thinking right now. Simple, are you crazy? You don't know the situation I'm in or the problems I have? That's true, I don't know the adversities in your life right now, but I do know the steps to success are simple.

The principles are easy to understand – the problem is implementation. Getting started and doing what needs to be done.

It's like trying to roll a big rock up the side of a hill. In the beginning, it seems impossible, but once you get some push and momentum going the rock rolls down the hill with ease. Achieving your goals is the same.

Getting started is the hardest part, but once you get going and build some momentum, it gets easier and easier.

In the end all you need to achieve success, whatever the word means to you, is to know what you want (goal) and take action every day to achieve it.

I don't care if you haven't a clue how you'll accomplish your goals. The key is to start moving towards them. When you start taking action and moving closer to your goals the how part will come. **Action is the prime principle of achievement.**

One could be stripped of all the advantages of life - money, job, vehicle, education and a support structure – yet still rise to greatness if they have a definite goal and take immediate, persistent, daily action to achieve it.

As you can see, the principles of success are easy to understand and very difficult to implement, because we let doubt, fear and inaction creep into our subconscious.

The only antidote for that is action. Don't stop to think how it will be done or if you can do it. Take action today and the next step

will appear tomorrow and the next day and so on until the goal has been reached.

Take one action at a time, step-by-step, and results will follow. You must take that leap of faith and keep your goals always in mind and heart. If you resolve to reach your goal no matter what and take persistent action, the way will be found to achieve it.

That's not pie in the sky thinking either. It's fact.

Setting around dreaming of a better life will not bring it to you. I don't give a crap how many affirmations you chant or how precise your visualizations are.

There's an old German proverb that states, *"God gave us the nuts, but he will not crack them for us."*

Visualization and affirmations are important to keep you focused and motivated, but action is what produces results, nothing else. A definite goal and persistent action bring about change. Visualizing and self-talk are tools, nothing more.

The modern self-help industry is making billions selling this lie. Setting around and thinking about things doesn't make it happen. No matter how much they preach you can achieve anything you want with relative ease, it just isn't true.

Sorry to burst your bubble here, but someone had to do it. Anything worthwhile having in life takes work and some struggle to achieve it. However, if you're doing what you truly want even the adversity will invigorate you.

If you take nothing else away from this book, remember this: **A definite purpose backed with persistent action is the only way to achieve anything in life.**

Wishing, hoping, dreaming and even praying will not do it. Success takes effort and action. If you aren't willing to do that, prepare to stay in the rut you've dug for the rest of your life.

Break free, achieve all your goals, live the life that you've imagined. Grab the brass ring by creating a definite goal and base your life on the action principle.

Remember, nothing happens without movement. Get moving towards your goals.

Your Life is Waiting

The life of your dreams is out there waiting for you. Will you take the steps needed to make it a reality or are you going to set there bitching and moaning?

Sorry to be so harsh, but I'm so tired of hearing people complain about how bad their life sucks, how God could do this to them and all sorts of lame, worn out excuses. God has nothing to do with your success or failure – you do.

Each individual has within the abilities and tools that can propel one from poverty to penthouse if they'd just take the first step and go for it. Life is about action, movement and doing.

Far too many people never, ever make a move towards their goals, or even set any for that matter. Then they whine and complain about how nothing ever works out.

We were put here to succeed. It's built into the very core of our being. But there are certain rules you must follow to win in this game of life. To learn a trade or put together a bike for your kid, you need to have an instruction manual or a teacher to show you the way.

The game of life is played that way. There are definite principles to achievement that practically guarantee the success you deserve. The key is to learn them, apply them and take

action. The learning part is easy. It's the doing and applying that trip people up.

We live in an age that is spoiled. The 'I want something for nothing crowd' is growing by leaps and bounds. Don't be one of those. The Universe gives you what you earn. It can't be any other way.

Sowing and reaping, cause and effect, like attracts like, is a universal law that you can't usurp. You might get away with it for a while, but in the end, it will exact its price.

You can achieve the life of your dreams and all the goals you've set for yourself. Just follow the Four Pillars of Success, work hard, practice gratitude with giving and enjoy the time you have here.

Success is within everyone's grasp, it is there for the taking. All one has to do is reach out and grab it.

Will you?

Epilogue

"I see only the goal. All obstacles must give way."

Napoleon Bonaparte

I kept the book short and sweet for a variety of reasons I would like to share with you.

First and foremost, I wanted to give you the meat and potatoes of these principles. I could have written 150, 200 or even 300 pages, giving examples as I went along, but it would have been all filler and fluff, without substance.

What I wanted to do was end all this confusion about what to do and how to do it. I wrote in a style that's plain. I'm not trying to be the next Michener or Dickens, my job is to hammer home ideas into your mind that will motivate and inspire you to action. If I have, I did my job. I don't need flowery speech or language.

Second, the sad truth is people are reading less and less, thanks in part to so much information being readily available everywhere. Cable and satellite TV, Ipods, Iphones, video games, and the Internet have caused an explosion of information being spread about at record speeds.

With that comes built in ADD. We need to filter this information coming into our brains and hence, our concentration and focus have suffered.

With a dwindling attention span and the proliferation of all things video, reading a book with plain old text has lost some appeal.

Don't be fooled by the small size though. This book is packed with all you need to achieve success in your life.

Whatever success means to you, however you define the term in your life, the tools and information you need to make it happen are right at your fingertips.

By following a proven formula that works, you can achieve a definite result, knowing without a doubt if you follow the formula success is assured.

Systems and formulas are used everywhere – from science and mathematics – to recipes and   business.

By following a proven formula that works, you can achieve a definite result, knowing without a doubt if you follow the formula success is assured.

This formula can be set down like an equation as follows:

The Lifestyle Success Formula:

$T + FO + FA + PA = Success$

T is target; FO is focus; FA stands for faith; PA is persistent action and that equals success in any field or endeavor.

The formula written out looks like this:

Target + Focus + Faith + Persistent Action = Success

You must have all of these in place if you want to reach your goals, aspirations and true potential.

Let's break it down further.

Target

Having a target or goal is the beginning of all achievement. If you don't know what you want, how do you expect to get anything?

Napoleon Hill was right on the money. This is the starting point of all riches. Set a goal, a target, some dream or purpose to pursue, and begin right now to make that dream a reality.

Know exactly what you want and nine times out of 10, you'll get it.

Focus

We are controlled by our dominant thoughts. What you think about expands. Therefore, it stands to reason if your thoughts are junk, your life is junk.

No matter what you call it: sowing and reaping; cause and effect; the law of attraction, it is a real force that governs the universe.

To make use of it requires focus and concentration.

Since dominant thought becomes your reality, doesn't it make sense to focus on what you want instead of what you don't want?

Faith

Faith or belief is next in line in the lifestyle success equation.

You must have confidence and a sincere belief that you will accomplish what you set out to achieve. Real faith is an assurance, an absolute belief, that what you want is coming to you right now – at this moment.

If you don't believe you can achieve your goal, if you can't see it in your mind's eye as already accomplished, you'll never receive it in the physical realm.

Persistent Action

Next to having a target or goal, this is the most important attribute to have in the lifestyle success formula.

As a matter of fact you could eliminate the others and still achieve most of your goals as long as you know what you want and take consistent, persistent action to get it.

It's that important.

All the hoping, fantasizing, visualizing, chanting affirmations and such is useless if you don't take action.

Action is the key to life. Nothing was ever accomplished without some form of action being taken. In order to achieve, you must do.

As the great Albert Einstein said, "Nothing happens until something moves."

If you don't move, your dreams are just that – dreams with no substance to them.

Set a target, focus on that target, believe you can achieve it, and begin to take action immediately until you reach your mark.

You can have, do or be anything in life if you follow the Four Pillars of Success. The key is you must live them. Remember applied knowledge is power. Information without action is nothing but dead words on a page.

Demand the impossible, dream your destiny. Follow the Four Pillars and live the life you were always supposed to have.

The Four Pillars of Success:

1. Know What You Want – Decide on a definite goal.
2. Focus – Keep the goal always in front of you.
3. Action – Nothing happens without movement.
4. Persistence – Never give up until the goal is reached.

I leave you with what could be the best success advice ever given. The following quotes are so subtle and profound. Absorb them into your consciousness until they're a part of you.

"Ask and it will be given to you; seek and you will find; knock and the door will be opened to you." – Matthew 7:7

"But as for you, be strong and do not give up, for your work will be rewarded." – 2 Chronicles 15:7

Take care and may success always be at your door.

About the Author

Brian Carson is an author, freelance sports writer and marketing consultant. He has been happily with his wife, Maria, for 22 years. Brian has a stepson Alex, who is living in San Diego with his beautiful wife Meyon and Brian's awesome grandson, Ryland. Brian is blessed with a loving and supportive family that includes his mother, Ada, David, his big brother, and his sister, Colette.

Brian has finished his second book, **Customers for Life,** this one on how small businesses can market themselves more effectively. In addition, Brian has various websites across the Internet.

He currently lives in Central Pennsylvania with Maria and his dog Spike.

www.ingramcontent.com/pod-product-compliance
Lightning Source LLC
Chambersburg PA
CBHW071639050426
42443CB00026B/739